THE ONLY WINDOW
THAT COUNTS

Deborah Keenan

THE ONLY WINDOW
THAT COUNTS

Deborah Keenan

Photographs by Timothy Francisco

New Rivers Press 1985

Some of the poems in *The Only Window That Counts* have previously appeared in the following publications: *WARM Journal*, *Minnesota Monthly*, *Pequod*, *New England Review/Breadloaf Quarterly*, *Milkweed Chronicle*, *The Poet Dreaming In The Artist's House* (Milkweed Editions), and *Passages North*. The author would like to thank the editors of these publications for permission to reprint here. The author would also like to thank Jim Moore, Don Brunnquell, Margaret Hasse, Margot Kriel, and Larry Sutin for editing assistance.

The Only Window That Counts has been published with the assistance of grants from the following organizations: the Arts Development Fund of the United Arts Council, the McKnight Foundation, and the First Bank System Foundation.

New Rivers Press books are distributed by

Bookslinger   and   Small Press Distribution, Inc.
213 East 4th St.   1784 Shattuck Ave.
St. Paul, MN 55101   Berkeley, CA 94709

The Only Window That Counts has been manufactured in the United States of America for New Rivers Press, Inc. (C. W. Truesdale editor/publisher, 1602 Selby Ave., St. Paul, MN 55104 in a first edition of 1000 copies.

This book is dedicated to
Stephen Seidel

THE ONLY WINDOW THAT COUNTS

Section I: No Replacement for Light

Section II: Grace

Section III: Good Dreams Or Milk

SECTION I
NO REPLACEMENT FOR LIGHT

TROUBLE

The most exciting movement in nature is not progress,
advance, but expansion, and contraction, the opening
and shutting of the eye, the hand, the heart, the mind.
We throw our arms wide with a gesture of religion to
the universe; we close them around a person.

Robert Frost

You have been traveling a long time and you are tired.
Eating meals with strangers, your hands linked around
a restaurant mug, no longer seems the right choice.
You have fought a long time to empty yourself

of want and need for any particular want or need,
you have reached for God diligently, while
what your hands possessed slipped away: the lover,
the father, the hand of one small child.

This particular spaceship is in trouble, and you're not
color-blind, you can see the red light flashing, all
those strangers running past you into the light. You have
held your hand open to God, you have been traveling a long time

and you are tired, you have closed your heart
because the pounding disturbed your sleep,
and the veins in your hands have retreated into your skin,
carrying a smaller burden of blood and tempo.

You are in trouble, and you're not color-blind,
and someone once told you in a time of candor that vacancy
would make you lighter, more acceptable to God's
liquid eyes but his hands seem full, and you've been carrying

11

these flowers for a long time, and you are used
to their weight; you know they can't open any wider
without a petal falling at last, and you are in trouble,
and you're not blind to the color of these flowers

and there is a right way to get off this spaceship,
and a right way to hold these flowers, and someone
told you once in a time broken apart with honesty that love
would weigh you down but might be worth it, make you acceptable

in your own eyes, and God's hands look so busy
from up here, he's a hard one to give flowers to,
and you're not color-blind and your hands have been almost
empty for a long time, except for the flowers that can't open

any wider.

WHAT MY DAUGHTER ASKED ABOUT THE ANGEL IN THE TREE

There's a mountain ash on fire outside the only window
that counts, and the children grow restless seeing
autumn is the end of things.

Why don't we let the angel of the tree inside?
We've got no money to leave home with,
and the architecture of our rooms spares us beauty
and little else.

Oh, let that angel in. This is no annunciation;
his wings are on fire, his sorrow is audible,
and we are cold enough to be useful,
lonely enough to be warmed.

EVERYTHING'S HURTING/DAUGHTER POEM

for molly megan keenan

a daughter who puts bandaids on water faucets
and on lions she names polly, white bandages wrapped
around legs of chairs, around china teacups; this kind
of daughter is the one i held out for, she's the easiest
joy i claim.

i think keats was her father. i think she could make
the frozen ones on the grecian urn come to life with
her fingertips, the frozen bride, the bold lover with mouth
of marble, suddenly warm, cold silence lifted.
she is friend to god, travels through his inner ear
seeking salvation for a mother who sins by not believing.

she is friend to zero, dog named after a number on his tag,
friend to slow ones in the stores, apologizes for my speed
through the lanes, explains to them why one of her doll's eyes
won't open, why the apple juice cries when we don't buy it.

i think she was born in devon. i think milk makes her
white inside, i think her color is green, her eyes gray
to make my father come back to life. i think she was born
to cancel out some pain i cannot stop from hurting.

FORMAL PRESENTATIONS OF LOVE

I.

The exchange of letters.

II.

The exchange of silence, which causes no fear, which we take for solace, which we take as a sign of a match, not one which kindles a small flame, to light a cigarette, or to purify a needle, signifies a match, which means it is easy to be silent together, which implies a closeness, which implies a chosen lack of words.

III.

The exchange of bodies, not like exchanging prisoners, where all are dressed in gray clothes, and their desire carries them across the line to their lost country, not like that, an exchange of bodies, a formal presentation of the lack of clothes, a formal presentation of skin, this hand rests above her head, clasping and releasing what is invisible, the air, just like her clothes, left in the hallway, left in a hurry, not wanting to be late for this formal presentation of love, which has the ordered familiarity of hold, then touch, then kiss, then touch lower, which has the formality of silence which implies a match, not like a small flame, but implies a match of silence, which is formal, like the exchange of letters, or of prisoners who long for their countries but cannot remember how to live there, once they cross the invisible line which divides the land, which feels like a wall one crosses over not knowing if there will be anyone there to meet, it has been years, dressed in old clothes, dressed in no clothes, not dressed, the hand resting on the white pillow, the hand touching the silent body, making a formal presentation of love, which implies a match, a lit cigarette, the time of gray light, which does not ease the formality of the presentation, which silence does not ease, which the hands do not ease, though they reach across white sheets, though one hand purified a needle once, lit a match once, wrote a letter once, more than once.

15

DECLARATION OF FEBRUARY

I see what brings this on. Orion no longer threatens
to drop his three-starred dagger,
he's just some stars without configuration or danger,

and the green plants which once taught the daily lesson
of turning to the source of light now only demand
water and drop leaf after leaf, giving away their grace.

This is what happens when the veils of beauty
lift from love, and rapture lifts too, away from the heart,
leaving no love, no beauty, only revelation of the ordinary,

what is no longer needed. The sun recklessly enters all my
windows
but it is the windows which speak of their own transparent
design,
not the heat, not the light of a day.

Flowers are everywhere this winter, white daisies
spin out of remembered orbit, masculine iris arrowing
into a heart, Scottish daffodils once wild and abandoned

under my careless feet, and finally, the dark roses, which have
lived in the offices of my heart, and in the regained austerity
of my bedroom; they have no thorns and I let them die,

die some more, I do not let them go.
I see what brings this on, all the controlled flowering
in the mildest of winters, while the children fly by

on sleds down private hills, bring their exhaustion home,
divide me, join me, even they have faltered
during this winter discussion in my ordinary soul.

But they come upstairs, scissors
bright and bloodless, red paper, white arrows,
I love you and I like you, litany of childhood,

St. Valentine colliding with one birth, St. Valentine
of the broken, pierced clean through heart, celebrated
in red, who died like all saints, leaving nothing behind

but ritual. I will go near no ocean now, would not risk
such simple movement toward remembered joy, February
protects me with a winter sky, and the snow makes

the stars brighter, but less ordered. The days
and nights pass with little regard for safety,
and we are all separate starlight unable to diminish the dark.

The sun is heat to her now, and the sea, water.

Rebecca Harding Davis

TWO WOMEN

for jean adams

two women stepped away from two men, left for the country where the snow was always clean, took their children for long walks and wild rides down hills even ethan frome would have thought twice about, dragged the children home on red and gold sleds, and all the children got warm again in the bathtub while the two women drank so much tea and hot chocolate in a blue house it's a wonder they could ever fall asleep, except they were tired from the walks and wild rides, from the long pull, their children's bodies snow encrusted heavy jewels swaying behind them, singing, "over the river and through the woods ..." until one woman laughed and one woman smiled, hearing the wild, "hurrah for the pumpkin pie," for the twentieth time that day.

two women stepped away from two men, let the children run wild new year's eve, wrapped them in their blankets, sang them to sleep, made a fire, played cards, and there were no bets, and nothing depended on either of them winning, and one woman listened to rock and roll for the first time, and one woman waited for her favorite songs, hungry for benedictions. and the air that night was not bitter, they fell asleep long before the bells rang, long before the other children in the countryside took to the streets, banging their mothers' pots and pans, celebratory noise to honor a year no one felt safe making even one prediction about, and the women made no resolutions, living weekend to weekend as they did, nothing was resolved, although it was a clear night, and the moon did its dance in the last december sky, and the stars were in place and full of myth.

two women stepped away from each other, and the future hung like twin stars, like a cold jewel between them, and one woman found her way back to the man she loved, and the two children were happy as they learned to reclaim the new version of an old life, and one woman left for a new world, and two children learned to follow her, knowing she would not let go of their hands.

two women left behind a blue house, where the air had always been sculpted by women, left behind fists smashed onto tables, and the idea of four children asleep in a room, black hair scattered next to gold and brown, two women left behind the idea of snow that one winter, that was always high and yielding, and rows of snowsuits, endlessly drying on radiators, and one drove away in a gold car, and one in a red car, back to an old city where their futures unfolded like laundry every new day, where all the white clothes slipped between their hands, reminding them of clean snow, and children, and one woman kept cooking, pots and pans scattered by a new baby, and one woman forgot she knew how to cook anything, and all the children were smart and beautiful and correct, and so were the two women.

DIVORCE

It takes a long intimacy, long and familiar inter-living before one kind of creature can cause illness in another.

The Lives of a Cell, Lewis Thomas

When Bob called to read aloud to me that day in the office, it felt just fine. I was busy being perfect in the old ways, shiny armor, dull pain. I felt all right in my hard chair that protected my back from the danger of too much gentleness. I think that was the day we talked about the comfort of magazines, and biographical notes in Esquire, that magazine for men and some women. When he read to me about how unnecessary it was for astronauts to be quarantined when they came home from the moon I laughed, having always known intuitively that moon germs would never cause my demise, so many other deaths readily available. I kept smoking as he read, and when he got to the line about "a long intimacy" I asked him to slow down, grabbed my pencil, copied the sentence in fast hard letters. I remember saying good-by, picking up my children after work, fighting with them in the grocery store about spending more quarters on football helmet and chicken hatching machines, tucking them in bed, and late that night throwing the quote into my notebook labeled, "Poems by others, Quotations collected, Poems of of mine which other writers have worked on, Remember to Edit."

Now it feels like years later. I have trouble being perfect in public because my friends laugh so hard when I try. There has been so much correspondence, that graceful letter from Paulette, with a reminder to be proud, and my friend David telling me to remember that the first time I got on a bicycle it felt like the least natural thing to be doing with my sense of balance. I remember laughing in agreement, crying later. I did love my white bike so much, sold it to buy college books about geology and logic. Now I don't ride bikes with hand brakes, because when I was pregnant I came down a winding hill on a ten-speed bike, panicked, squeezed the brakes with my wet hands, and hurtled over the handlebars into a pond, landing between two swans who were stunned by my arrival.

I'd like to be proud of all the things I've resolved never to learn how to do, as if to prove that everything I know how to do is enough, and it's time to rest. I keep thinking of intimacy, and astronauts disappearing into the face of the moon. I was reminded by my friend Jim the other day that I thought I'd been divorced five years, but it had only been three. Then I was out buying my mother a valentine present, and I talked to the clerk about my son who was in fourth grade, and she said she'd assumed I was one of the college kids, out for a Saturday walk. So I came home and looked into the mirror for a while, remembering my mother's advice to start now with the face cream, before it's too late. I wanted to call out for blessings to descend into the hearts of all my friends. I wanted to drop to my knees and ask for something important for all of us who try to love carefully, who think too much, who try to stop our hands from breaking someone else's dreams, or from making shadows on someone else's face. There's that wild, holy feeling that comes over me; I never made it to my knees, but I thought about divorce, and intimacy, and illness, how it blossoms like splendid poisoned roses in all the story books. I wanted protection for everyone. I wanted all the astronauts to come home, leave the sky alone, to come out of quarantine and walk down ordinary roads, ridding themselves of weightlessness and the human desire to fly away from those we used to love.

ROCK AND ROLL DESTINY

I. We are not prisoners of rock and roll. We are volunteers.

Peter Wolf, J. Geils Band

II. Badlands, you gotta live 'em everyday, let the broken hearts stand, it's the price you gotta pay ...

Badlands, Bruce Springsteen

III. With only you and what I've found,
we'll wear the weary hours down.

Rose Darling, Steely Dan

I.

They find each other accidentally. A turn of conversation, a line from a rock and roll song slips from the other's mouth; suddenly that mouth is desired. The sign, dead giveaway, one raw, unyielding cynic left over from the sixties collides with another. It won't be pretty but it won't be dull.

II.

It's not that simple. Never was. The badlands only a partial landscape, prisioners in some ways, they can never be sure whose heart is breaking and whose is only bending. They both know beginnings and endings are the only things that count in rock and roll, and they've never been the types to figure out what goes in between the passion and the swift fall from desire, though they've done it over and over again. In rock and roll, doing it more than once means little; you try not being a professional about it but it comes naturally, with the territory.

III.

That's what they'd like it to mean sometimes. That continuity might imply something besides boredom, submission to the ordinary. The constant battle in the rock and roll heart, to seek, find, hold dear, to recklessly change and mean it, to stop growing smaller, less able to love. They're read too many books, watched the hearts fall like snow, like a hand let go of, gracelessly dropping to someone's side. They are volunteers, keep playing the songs, let the tapes carry the dark, charged message of connection; somewhere inside themselves they agreed to live like this. It works a few hours a week, they keep letting the music count, it's a sin, a way to live.

SWANS

Cutting the swans free was the easy job. They all knew the storm was building. They could see it move, county to county, then reach the other side of the lake. She couldn't understand why she wasn't asked to take the laundry in, that was a hard job, strung on many white clotheslines, poles anchored on either side of the canal, clothes dancing like ghosts, barely reachable, as people leaned from either side of the water to pull them free into the baskets. The cabins on shore already looked restless, as if they wanted to blow away just from spite. The summer people were frightened but competent. When they told her to cut the swans free they gave her a hatchet. She preferred scissors, but there was not time and the rope was thick. The swans were tethered together, tied around their necks and then to each other. They were a group, not just three swans, or six, maybe nine or thirteen, and the rope, though fairly tied, would choke them if the wind threw them against the wall of any cabin. Cut free, they could bob together through the wild waves, tied to each other but not to the spike one of the summer visitors had hammered deep into the ground at the beginning of the season. The hatchet was easy to hold. She swung it once and the ends of the rope pulled apart from each other, swiftly unravelling until the ends were like horses' manes. The swans drifted away from shore. She watched them for a long time, riding the lake's waves like white messages someone had remembered to send to a lover after too much silence, after that time when certainty turns only to hope, but before the dull vacancy sets in and completes the absence. Cutting the swans free was the easy job, and the wind was exceptional, and she felt the shoreline wouldn't be complete without her standing there.

SUNDAY EVENING

When light falls so hard after such clarity,
after wild storms, when light leaves,
harsh, harsh, some punishment felt;

you're made to pay for the mind's leaps,
for the pulls you feel away from a life,
where's the day, the night before, when it was clear too,

in the midst of rain and skin on white sheets,
when blackbirds refuse to speak or move one eye
to stop the Sunday thoughts, when gardens grow

orderly, with precision, defeating the wild
and passionate sowing, when the air is this correct,
and the night this sudden; time takes his toll

so carefully, carrying you in his hand,
he had seemed so tempered, going with you all that way,
but he's just a vengeful god without heart, so many disguises

you think you are lost from him, then his uncanny finger
pencils into you, harsh probe, pushing you on.
To remember this is your own life, this Sunday night,

some needed addition that defeats the personal clocks
swinging pendulums through once empty forests,
the tick tick of responsibility, the beat of a heart

flying at a clock to change its rhythm. Sometimes
living so close to a forest seems the only right thing
to do, you want to see some controlled vision

of uncontrolled nature, want to believe with every walk
you might get lost and lost again, want to believe
clocks in the forest are more quiet,

more acquiescent to what is needed on Sunday evening
when life is possibilities you dream
of not discarding in the darkness.

GRIEF

Someone who is about to be left alone again,
And can no longer stand it.

Edward Hopper and the House by the Railroad/1925, Edward Hirsch

This will have to stand for grief, this arrangement
outside my window, children playing that old statue game,
and the girl who's just no good at it.
When the leader yells "Freeze!" she's too liquid,
can't claim whatever shape she's hovering near.
I want to be that girl on the dark green lawn
who cannot hold her position. When you leave me
again my mouth will be open, screaming, my legs
running in your direction. And I don't even want
to stop you, only desire my composure shattered,
my body not held in check. I want to be calling
you back with all the codes broken, so you will
know the grief is alive and not considered.

BELONGING TO GOD

Momentary exhilaration. You are fuller than your body can stretch, yet the skin holds. When my children belong to God I am caught by their easy giving over to ownership. My daughter calls from the bedroom that God has slipped his hand inside her red curtains, she tells me he's rearranged the dolls, the stuffed rabbit is mended, the ribbons have lost their knots, their tangled union. I'm in the kitchen and don't know what to do with the information. The knife doesn't slip. Dinner will be eaten on time, the time I say.

When my father talked of destiny I never thought of God, only of piano lessons arched over my life, umbrellas made of music, thought my fingers would always know the way to touch the white keys. I imagined baseball games I'd win alone, complacent champion, summer dust sifting into my tennis shoes, touching home. I thought of my brain cells multiplying in my skull, each new cell carrying truth, more lessons. I knew I needed all the facts there were to fulfill the luck of my own life.

My son called to me that God was inside his red fire engine. He wanted to show me. I did move as fast as I could, spilling like water through the kitchen door into a summer day, but God had left by the time I got there, my son smiled, told me I'd missed him by seconds.

Belonging to God took a lot of time when I was young. Praying right, the knot of fingers, hymns to be memorized, saying no to hot boy hands in backseats, trying to remember I belonged to God in those backseats took time.

Baptized at twelve, in white, the small of my back supported by a man's arm as he bent me backwards under water. It seemed like a sin to stand there in white, dripping on the carpet, it seemed like a sin not to feel I belonged to God when I went under the water like that, so many clothes on, my heart wide open and alert.

My daughter explained once, in the backseat of my car to her cousins, how to get God to come to you. "Two people sit very close, and they send their breaths into each other's mouths, back and forth, and their breaths get smaller and smaller and suddenly God is inside their mouths."

The music is strong today and everything seems sacred, the circles under my eyes, how green summer is, how rarely the sun shines these months, how rarely I go under water. Everything seems sacred, the hard music, my children belonging to God, how language tries to be correct, wants to be holy, fails, how music is the only thing I can stand under my skin, the only thing breaking into my heart, everything seems sacred, even not belonging to God feels sanctified.

FOLDS OF WHITE DRESS / SHAFT OF LIGHT

The Annunciation

Peter Paul Rubens, 1577-1640

She had been reading, that much we know.
An empty vase beside her book, no one in this story
thought to bring her flowers.

The angel's cape is flame, his hair gold fire.
One more angel drops from heaven barefoot, the shoemakers sigh.
He is fine, and his gray wings match his outfit.
She is dressed for a dinner party and he flies through
the window, drops to his knee, beseeches her to accept
the offer. She listens but her hands are placed
on the canvas in shapes of rejection.

She would like to lift her eyes to the baby
angels floating near the ceiling.
She would like to catch the dove in her raised hand.
She may be glad the shaft of light turns her white dress
holy, she may not.

She worries: where can one place a beautiful man
angel at the dinner table, who can make small talk
with him, or offer polite inquiries about celestial weather?

She understands babies, even floating ones,
and she wants the dove to stay near her,
that much is clear, and it is also apparent
her blue cloak cannot protect her from god's
demand, or the strong hand reaching
toward her, about to make her famous
and pregnant.

NO REPLACEMENT FOR LIGHT

I.

Even when times were easy, there was no replacement for light. I'd talk then of statues, how their stone smiles beckoned. I thought those were holy moments, carved from inflexible time. Margaret, the virgin martyr, clasped stone hands on her younger sister's shoulders, pulled her into the sea with an abandoned sureness that what God had in store was safer than the advancing soldiers. St. Cecilia placed her hands in the sign of the trinity, gave herself over to her pure and ferocious lover, Jesus, then turned to white marble in front of the eyes of people on their way to market, or a wedding. The light from the marble glorified the street.

II.

There is no replacement for light. Wind drove me wild inside two nights ago and I cried for a lover to hold me, but I am cold now, and every window has become a frozen landscape of a dream I've had. I am sick of the sun burning and making no difference; in the moonlight cutting through the windows I see only white arms of children signalling for rescue in the snowdrifts but I am alone in the car; the brakes are faulty. The windows hold the false stained glass of history, but I want their cold that seals me in like claimed property. There's no leniency in my blood lately, and my hands are carved at my sides, too heavy to lift for an embrace.

III.

Sometimes I want Margaret's sister to break from the pure stone hands, to resist the icy waves, the thoughtless virginity. Tonight, the moonlight turned the frost to lace, and Cecilia's hands rose from the sign, and cooled my forehead. I slept without bitterness inside a memory of summer.

THE NEXT POEM

For Jim Moore

Perhaps the light will prove another tyranny.

The Windows, Cavafy

You said it might have something to do with oceans,
then it was the quick drive home, and someone else's
schedule to follow, and now it's another week
and I'm still fighting off winter with clanking radiators
and old sweaters I can't give up to Good Will.

You said it might have something to do with oceans,
or one ocean, maybe, I can't remember exactly,
and then it was the drive home and taking out two keys
for two locked doors, and inside the first door
was a white dog covered with blood and I stepped over him.

You said it might have something to do with an ocean,
and I didn't feel like going straight home, the keys
are always in my purse because I never lose them,
and the dog is better now, his white fur coming back
to white, and the wound will heal in time.

You said it will have something to do with oceans,
and I thought of traveling with you, and all the water
the two of us have seen in our double lives,
sometimes leaving you is as hard as leaving
a lover, and sometimes it's harder than that.

You said it will be about an ocean, I remember now,
and I was grateful for the clue, have been too full
of other voices lately, my own voice only full of answers:
"your hat's in the hallway, yes, I love you, yes, I'll read
a chapter of *Heidi*, no, I don't have time to help you build a rocket."

You said it will be about an ocean, but of course
it's about you instead, my friend, you, the ocean,
full of treasure and shine, light and depth,
and it's about keys too, and not wanting to go home
and winter too, all the windows I look out of,

about a white dog covered with blood, that surprise
I got going home to a place where I thought I knew
every detail, and it's about how I never lose my keys,
and about Heidi too, who loved the mountains like
I love the ocean, and about oceans, yes, oceans.

BE GOOD

Today I heard a story about a priest,
and watched my children be good for hours,
and I was good too, and felt goodness
taking its usual toll, felt the old ambivilance
slide under my skin.

Today I heard a story about a priest,
a good priest who went when called,
to old parishoners, to crazy bishops,
with no care he kept going, always pulled
from bed or prayer, coming and going too many times
a day, for goodness, and he gave that goodness away
until his good heart broke open and he died, good and young.

Today I felt like being bad for many weeks,
wanted my children to watch me, these children,
destined to be good, wanted to sweep that goodness
out of them, feeling the old tracks they're on are
too set, too shiny for them to ever step off.

Today I thought of childhood girlfriends, Lori, Kathy, Kristine,
all of us brought up on *Little Women*, how all of us would,
after the Beatles records were put away at night,
talk about goodness, and sometimes beauty and goodness,
and which we would choose if we could only have one.

Be good, I say to my children every day, never telling
them to be beautiful, though they are both.
Be good, I say to myself, good like a priest,
be good in huge swirls of time, year after year
of sweeping, spinning canvases of goodness, yes,
be good today because badness has such energy
it can drive the goodness from your soul
and leave you bad, even if you've practiced
goodness, and have been walking down the road
to grace all your life.

SECTION II
GRACE

*Some also have wished that the next way to their
father's house were here, and that they might be
troubled no more with either hills or mountains
to go over, but the way is the way, and there is
an end.*

The Pilgrim's Progress, Part II, John Bunyan

GRACE

What is grace?

Almost always in summer. In sunlight and heat you pass pleasure on your left, work on your right, on your knees for hours it begins to make sense. The pile of weeds, steady, growing, this holy garden, annuals, perrenials, sweet peas buried so deeply in May you winced at the instructions, drove a stake through the seed packet, marked the row with disbelief.

Who decides?

Someone better than you. Someone older than you. Someone for whom sacrifice was appalling yet done without thinking.

What is God?

Something better than you. Something older than you. Someone for whom sacrifice was appalling, something done without thinking, something with claws or wings, an unrecognizable heart.

Why this anger?

Because the claws dig and dig, because the seed has been planted too deep. Because disbelief is followed by flowers.

When does the journey start?

I have been on this train too many generations to count. The idea of me, face smudged and smoky, retreats backwards on old photographs until the idea of cameras is absent. My face created by too many women to count.

What is grace?

Almost always in winter. Dark days, the sun setting before you've acknowledged the light. Eyes tired from too much studying, bookmarks in the wrong places. Seedbooks lie scattered; whatever you're planning in the dark feels non-essential, and the feeling you're holy was created through desire, therefore poisonous.

Must you eat?

Eating is like imagination. You haven't learned to stop eating, either.

Must you starve?

I have imagined I must starve. To create the desire to starve undoes the good of starving. Starving without thought appeases even a brilliant appetite.

Why remain outside?

Not vanity. Not pride. To remain outside is conscious, to see oneself outside is powerful, lonely, hardly reckless. To remain outside is to make a show, the last cardinal, pretending he forgot to fly south, eager for his red wings to flame against snow, the mother calling the little daughter, "Come and see the beautiful cardinal, there, no, there, see where I'm pointing."

Why write of angels?

Because it was easy. You knew all about them. What it's like to float between homes, to be the messenger, to feel immortal yet caught. A persona in honor of the death in your life.

Why believe?

Because we are mortal. Mortal and afraid. Because we have imagination, because we have no imagination. Because home means so much that to leave it for less than eternal life means selling out too cheaply.

Where is comfort?

I used to say: a window of my own and the empty bed. In the wine, in the wafer. In black books, in cut flowers.

What is grace?

Almost always in summer. Growing up without palm trees, nature so manageable, you are on your knees because your father wanted you to be good at controlling nature, and you traveled so fast past pleasure and the idea of work you intrigued him for awhile. Almost always in summer. You could travel through order into heat, through heat into light, though you understood gravity, you dreamt of wings.

What is emptiness?

The absence of imagination. To imagine emptiness creates it falsely.

What is gravity?

It was invented to keep you in your place. A law. Gravity pulls babies out of you, hooks you to a floating planet, it is full of power and imagination, usually a man, often a mother, always something you have been taught you cannot do without.

Where is the finish?

No response. The cardinal stays all winter. He didn't forget to fly south. He wasn't supposed to. Never lie about things that can fly.

What is God?

Something with so much color we can't see him. Someone with enough imagination to make lizards and roses and gravity and babies.

What began this?

Someone who wasn't hungry ate an apple. Someone who was desperately hungry ate an apple, was taught shame, and had to leave home. Someone who thought she was hungry picked an apple, stepped over a snake without noticing hm, and thought of leaving home. Someone without shame received it as a gift, and became deeply powerful and ashamed after eating. Someone who looked like Rapunzel and who loved the idea of apples started it.

Why a son?

Because women had so much power men had to learn to hate them. Because every man wants a son. If a virgin had produced a daughter, someone would have driven a stake through her heart, buried them both so deep they could never have turned to flowers.

Why this anger?

It tastes like food, and I haven't learned to starve myself. It feels like gravity, keeps me from floating off the planet.

Why this longing?

Belief is so beautiful to watch. When it belongs to others I see more clearly. Longing is as close as I come to emptiness; I don't know what I long for and my imagination cannot help me.

Why water?

An obsession with cleanliness. Everyone has a memory of water, something universal, easy to contemplate near the ocean, easy to desire near the desert. When in water we feel lighter, less attracted to gravity or flowers.

What is grace?

Almost always an emptiness. A deeply felt lack of imagination. An availability. A reverence for absence.

Who decides?

Prophets and martyrs. Children caught by angels while out walking. Children who do not speak in metaphors.

What is God?

He is a huge hole in the sky and he fills it. He is someone who wouldn't write a book, or would write one book only, non-fiction. He has no friends.

Why this anger?

I must constantly invent what can fill the hole in the sky. Sleeping is necessary, yet there's the fury of lost hours. Because when I sleep I dream of the hole in the sky, filling it over and over, breaking the rules of saints and martyrs.

Why water?

When we are in water all we want is to stay in water. We do not suddenly want love or children or change. If we can remember not to want it too much, we begin our memory of the journey while submerged.

What is grace?

Almost always in summer. You, the uncoiled spring. You cannot be a jack-in-the-box. Heat prevents any mechanical cleverness.

Must you eat?

You must eat. Or, you must not eat. You wonder why your father taught you to be a gardener. You ate flowers, but more often you stole the new peas, or the raspberries. You learned about food and guilt in the garden, the pail half-empty; you don't remember blaming it on the birds who floated down from the hole in the sky each summer. You just said, "I got tired of picking the berries."

When does the journey start?

It starts in sleep and ends there. It starts when you notice people have eyes and carry flowers.

Must you starve?

I must know how to starve and then do it or not. I must know how it's done and not talk about it. The words fill me up again, just when I almost had the knack of starving without involving my imagination.

Why remain outside?

Where else to be in summer? You were once trapped in an elevator. You once imagined you were trapped in an elevator and your claustrophobia became a work of art. Inside is warmer than outside, even in summer. If you don't brag about it, there is holiness outside.

Why write of angels?

Because they are sexless and provocative. They do not sleep, and in not sleeping they do not dream of flight. Even awake, they do not dream of flight, they dream of gravity. We all want what we cannot have.

Why believe?

We cannot accept our mortality. There is nothing else to leave the children except money. The longing to be holy makes us weep, and we trust tears since they are made of water and come from our body, a double blessing.

Where is grace?

In the unread book.

What is empty?

The babies are empty. The cup is not empty. The winter is empty, except for the buzz of imagination at the windows.

Where is grace?

In the throat of the lily.

What has gravity?

Grown-ups. Gardens. Crosses. Electric lights that let us see in the dark when we should be sleeping.

What is God?

Someone with so little imagination he deals only in facts.

How do we finish?

At random. Choking on something we can't swallow. Claw marks on fragile hearts. A father's fist, a mother's love. A train, a plane, disappearing into fire.

What is God?

The idea of fire. Something older than me. Autumn leaves and the last chrysanthemums before the emptiness of winter.

Why a son?

A son is an image of the father. Half the world received a mirror. The rest of us have a virgin, a martyr on fire, or witches.

Why baptism?

Because it is cold fire, and we do not die from it. Since it is not fire we feel safe. Since it is water we feel cleansed.

Why incense?

I have never understood incense.

What would surprise you?

To not meet an angel. To grow wings. To be born again as a cardinal, caught forever in snow.

What have you seen?

The doubt in the gardener's eyes. The heat of summer and what it controls. The flowers rising from God's hands. The bright scissors, the imagined bouquet.

Why the thorns?

Unpredictable pain is more surprising. God created them not for roses only, but for the holly. The virgin, the baby, the stepfather were swallowed once by holly and learned to count on God's goodness. God is a gardener with a deep imaganation and no fear of drama.

Must you eat?

You must not eat roses. You must eat if you know what it means to swallow.

Must you starve?

When you were swimming you wanted no food. When you were reading you got hungry. When the mother called the little daughter to the table it sounded like bells ringing, but she couldn't leave the garden that whole summer.

Why a cross?

Because stepfather and father were carpenters. Wood burns, but it floats on water. The shape was useful to the purpose: how else to pierce the gentle hands?

What is grace?

To perceive doubt and call it holy. To wait in a garden and not call out for a friend.

Who decides?

Priests and saints and women who know the ocean.

What is God?

A man created in our image. A prayer without imagination.

When did the journey start?

A woman on her knees in a garden forgot she wasn't hungry. A woman was seduced by the beauty of apples. A woman gave herself up to summer.

Why remain outside?

Not bravery. Not happiness. She said, "It is so beautiful outside." She said she knew the names of all the flowers, little liar, she said she built a home of snow and the sun melted the door closed. She imagined she would die because her father was at work, but her brothers heard her crying. She was born a girl, but has the hands of a gardener.

Must you eat?

Food is comforting, but you are an unimaginative cook. You believe in the work you do, food is fuel, not sin.

What is emptiness?

The presence of grace. Gentle hands that hold no flowers. A white candle lit, not for effect, but for holiness.

What is gravity?

Imagining your father was a gardener. Food. Friends. A lover. False compassion. Train tracks and pride.

Where is the end?

Not over a hill or mountain range. Perhaps in the kitchen, your hands busy keeping things clean.

Why this anger?

A child walked into her house at the wrong time, was handed over to the men who thought she was too happy for her own good. Beauty is a false god, but she was not responsible for all the beauty she saw.

Why this longing?

The children are holy. The children have begun to create beauty and to love it. I was empty once and the memory is a claw against my heart. My hands want more than to be tangled up in beauty. My father is dead and I cannot turn him into a white rose, though I try.

Why remain outside?

To go inside means your heart will be seamless again, and you have grown proud of the scar. You will know your father again, and it has been so peaceful here in the garden, growing flowers in his honor without lifting your eyes.

Must you starve?

You were getting good at it. This decision to swallow God lacks humility. You cannot swallow what is incomprehensible. Either eat or starve, without charm.

What is grace?

A glass of water, candles lit for light, the history of thorns, the angel who doubts, hands that take no pride in gentleness.

What have you seen?

Enough beauty. Enough drama. A gardener I knew once grew a rose with no thorns, but his hands were full of lilies and I turned away.

What have you heard?

Flowers being cut with silver scissors. Summer ending.

What is God?

The cardinal outside the window. The wrong man to give your heart to. A flame you thought could only burn you once. Children on fire.

Why this anger?

All this, and more. The train, the body in the wind, the shotgun blast, the broken child, the cleverness of God.

Why this longing?

It is cold. It is not summer. The holy candle.

What is grace?

Almost always. The children. The journey. The open book. The empty heart. The house made of snow. The pierced hands. The doubt. The garden in autumn. The cardinal's wing. The disbelief. The flowers.

SECTION III

GOOD DREAMS OR MILK

GOOD DREAMS OR MILK

Still impossible to kiss the child,
and not see the child explode.

Cantata At Midnight, Charles Baxter

private retreats and public disorders
are in full view now; after a long season
without new life babies ride inside friends
or burn whole into lives, altering paths we'd been lingering on.

there are mouths to feed. my children's faces
are private candles i sometimes worship at, the touch of
their skin, the implicit blessing that comes when children
are desired, and children are being born again, while the world
lurches in a fouled orbit, tampering with private pledges
made in the night by new lovers, and with lullabies being sung
all over town:
>   pony boy, pony boy, won't you be my pony boy?
>   and:
>   sweet and low, sweet and low, winds of western seas.
the hush hush words about mockingbirds,
rings without stain,
soft words before sleep,
the comfort of new skin and old songs.

such privacy by gold light cannot outshine the polished guns,
the accomplished liars, the diplomats flaming at the last gates
in every city, easter won't stay, palm fronds fade
and children's new clothes are put away with trembling hands
by lovers who bend to kiss the faces of children,
or to hear the daughter's voice: oh, i've needed you so much today,
weary, as if laying claim to some sin.

and the big world's chapter and verse drone on,
and children are flying apart
and hands cannot reach
fast enough to stop their small, quiet disintegration.

we are here again, we say to each other,
while the children tangle in sheets,
call out for good dreams or milk,
and we pull the blankets up, hungry for them
to wake up alive.

THE ROW OF NASTURTIUMS

The nasturtiums do not die.
If you need them to die
you hit them with a hoe.
The leaves do not die,
if you need them to die
tear them from their stems,
use them as coasters,
use them to play cards
with all your color-blind friends,
if you need them to die, use them.

The leaves are lily pads:
you note the absence of frogs,
the absence of the lilies themselves;
the leaves are the green hearts
of a pagan garden. You would play
Solitaire with these hearts,
you would play *Oh Hell* and break
the heart of the banker.

The power resides in the leaf,
veins so clear in triangular networks,
and I've seen it all in the green hearts today.

And the flowers, they're not lilies
stunned by a dream of purity, nasturtiums
have brilliant petals, tight baby fists
born from color wheels out of control,
lurking under those mandala leaves.

The nasturtiums do not die.
The zinnias gave up to gray,
and I pulled the cosmos out before
their time, making room for bulbs
I barely trust, and the chrysanthemums
won't beat the hard luck frost this time,
and my heart is in the garden
with the row of nasturtiums,
the most careless seeds
I ever scattered. No one ever told me
how they love to live.

WHAT HE LIKED HE HAD A LOT OF

For Dick Francis

Ushered into the backyard, you see one thousand
peonies, one thousand for sure, at least, only pink,
and she raises her hand in an arc, and her arm bends
like the stem of a peony under the weight of bloom,
she says: what he liked he had a lot of.
Though he died many years ago, no other flowers
have been added to this hidden English garden.
It's too many to praise, too many to ignore.

She takes you inside and you don't say a word:
every space on every wall holds a painting
of a sailing ship, or, many sailing ships,
or ships in harbor, or a ship at sunset.
"Oh, look," you say, "here's a ship up on shore."
Painted men are repairing it, high noon and glossy.

She takes you out through the back yard,
the interview complete, lets you out the gate,
her eyes ride your sloping shoulders down
the old street.

So many blossoms, so many sailing ships;
the world feels cramped and unsteady.
You walk quickly, claustrophobic, your stomach
at sea without you, the peony in your lapel
full-blown and gaudy, a tiny clown's wig
riding on your breast, you, the one who've
never liked more than one of anything.

OLDER WOMEN IN MY LIFE

My women are aphoristic, say things like: "independent as a hog on ice," and these women might have been atheists, but they speak Hebrew, or carry rosaries; they have lives which hold me, and I forget they have done stupid things with their children, or left the convent, and their houses, some of them, have burned down around them, and they managed to save their blue taffeta dresses, and maybe a beautiful oval hand mirror, and the brush that matches the mirror, though I've never understood how it could get through any hair, no matter how thin, how fine.

They saved many things escaping from the fire, and my son's tape recorder preserves little. My mother used to dress for parties at the country club, green taffeta and jade earrings and an engagement ring with an emerald, and her perfume was dense and almost filled the room with smoke as she bent over my small face to kiss me good-night, and I would hear her rustle away down the hallway, all that moving green and then the red hair on top, and the beautiful red mouth saying, "good-night, darling, sleep well, good-night," and I suppose I dreamt of her dancing, or brushing her hair softly in the powder room where all the prettiest women always disappeared.

During those years I had only two older women in my life, Augusta, my neighbor, who walked with one crutch, who was surprised every year in the same way, with the same words by the May basket I left on her doorknob; and my grandmother Maud, who was so mysterious in her deafness I never knew her, but became intimate with her house, her bed, her dishes, how if I sat up high on the porch swing at night I could see the temple glowing in Salt Lake City, and I knew that was where my beautiful mother went to dance because there was no place else pretty enough for her.

THE TREES

For Pat and Tim

(When the little girl was asked, "And what do you like best
about the State Fair?" she said, "The trees.")

Winners in beauty, in talent, in patient congeniality.
The trees stay up, the trees change colors, the trees grow
and make rings to wear for birthdays.
This tree bears fruit, this tree breaks the heart, this tree
opens all eyes to possibilities.
This tree won the amateur talent contest
   singing *Flow Gently Sweet Afton.*
This tree won for beauty, the judges rooted to their chairs,
a unanimous ballot.
This tree was a friend, turned his back on jealousy,
   gave shade in the heat wave.
The trees at the fair avoid games of chance and never travel.
The trees at the fair are quiet, the horses and lop-eared rabbits
watch them from the open air barns; they can never meet.
The trees at the fair have green hearts, open hands, they wait
and watch, they own nothing, they are not prideful, they make no
false moves, they bend away from neon, they do not know how
to love themselves, they love the girl who loves the trees.

APPLES

Loving apples the way she did, anything was possible.
She might lean out any window, she might take an apple
from a passing perfect stranger. She was all right
about that, having trusted the world for years, she
included all passers-by in that bond. She wasn't hazy,
sharp black hair, and the white skin not from pallor,
just from contentment indoors, where she could arrange
her possessions, plan a party, cut hearts from red
wrapping paper for St. Valentine's Day, eat a lot
of popcorn while waiting. She was a pretty normal
woman, all in all, wore brown skirts, tied her hair
back when it bugged her, wore a vest four days a week.
She had a clock in the shape of a circle and it never
ran down. She knew just when to go to the window
without looking at the hands. She had no small friends,
she knew how to be happy whether it was Golden Delicious,
Winesap, Jonathan, McIntosh or Beacon that was given
to her. She liked apples more than anything, more
than love or dreams or things. And the world opened
to her; like apples, she stored herself in cold, dry
places, was hearty, had a tart, piercing taste. She
believed in apples and stayed in good health. She did
not glow, but the apples shone for her.

STAYING AFLOAT

A nice tall glass of water with no ice inside, or maybe
just the very heart of a head of lettuce. Maybe
this year no one getting cut while carving the face into
a pumpkin. A good statue that no one else has found might
make it happen, or just a can of vegetable beef soup without
so much barley filling it up. Maybe not going to Florence
but having a really complete dream of it, or your son
catching so many fish he finally stops worrying about his lures.
Stamps without American flags could carry you a long way
to this place, or no grocery shopping for months. Maybe
moving everyone who knows your phone number to a secret
country without telephone wires, or just all the telephone
poles dressed like scarecrows for amusement and separation.
No more birds, less need for sleep. Everyone who wonders
if they want children gets them, but they're returnable if
it doesn't work out. A nice new set of sheets, or a strike
by the bookkeepers at your bank, money flowing like silk
off the bolts. No more drive-through arrangements at fast food joints,
and everybody out walking with enough strollers
for all the babies so their arms don't get jerked quite so
often. Plenty of apples, enough wind, windows that stay open,
and a calm and easy relationship with desire.

THE AMATEUR

Whenever a celebrated murder occurred Bolden was there at the scene drawing amateur maps. There were his dreams of his children dying. There were his dreams of his children dying. There were his dreams of his children dying.

Coming Through Slaughter, Michael Ondaatje

In seventh grade geography we colored maps.
The continent of Africa was assigned when I
was in my red period. Each exotic country
challenged my crayons, my sense of harmony.
Cardinal red, plum, violet for the African
flowers on my mother's window ledge, wine,
the dark continent blossomed under my
steady left hand. Never before have so
many stars risen at the top of my work.
A true amateur, I colored for love.

An amateur parent at twenty-one, I was in
my blue period, to match my son's eyes and
the heaviness in my heart. His infant kabuki
hands defined the air, my dreams grew unsteady
as he grew more beautiful. I charted elaborate
plans for my life without him, while he dreamt
of clowns coming through the window to scratch
his eyes, and so we painted clowns, coloring
in details of anonymous faces, red stars on
flat white cheeks, blue triangles over empty
eyes. He slept easier then, while I dreamt
of masked men pushing him through the bedroom
window after disconnecting the stereo, severing
the telephone chord.

When my daughter in her dark beauty arrived
I longed for hours of dream-filled sleep,
but she upset the mapping out I did for her
future with illness, her unsteady breathing
became the rhythm of my nights, for a year
all nights were broken, and she and I did
the rocking chair dance and far away in Africa
civil wars changed the names of half the countries
I had colored, believing they would never be altered.

It doesn't matter how many scientists explore
the country of sleep. It doesn't matter that
police draw white chalk lines around bodies
violently dispatched to eternity. Nothing
defines absence, there are no colors to choose
from when drawing in the shapes of missing
children, and when they slip away as you hold them,
or disappear under car wheels, or swim too far
in your dreams of water there are no rescues
plotted, the god of dreams is malevolent,
a professional, and you have done it all
for love, the competition is fixed, and the dream
of death is the first blossom after a child
blooms under your skin.

WHEN IT TURNED INTO FICTION

There was marriage, some lawn-mowing,
there was a night trip down the river,
lights of the river towns like gold
costume jewelry, clustered or strung.

Autumn came, and the morning glories
still blurted open each morning, hot pink
or blue eyes trapping the small white trellis
with the hard look of ownership and longevity.

There was the first storm of winter
where everyone you knew got home safely,
and you didn't care how early in November
it was; exceptional beauty was falling from the sky.

In the months that followed things got worse.
Many messages arrived from warm places, one friend
after another left town, the postcards were all funny.
You were busy at home, a baby coming, snow to shovel.

When it turned into fiction you were standing
in the kitchen. You had asked your mother
to make some oatmeal cookies and she had
but they weren't enough. Nothing was.

So you began to bake your own batch.
Everything was all right until you found out
there were no raisins. After you cried for a while you became
more intelligent. The thought of going to the store

was out of the question: the cold, the ice.
You dumped a box of Raisin Bran into a wedding bowl,
you picked out the raisins one at a time
until your recipe was complete.

You were not yourself that whole morning.
You burnt only one tray of cookies.
It was cold and no one you knew was home
and you hadn't dialed the phone for weeks anyway.

Fiction is like this.

WHAT TO THINK ABOUT
AFTER THE BABY COMES

We are on a first name basis with too many fictional characters.

Stephen Seidel

Elise and Carla and Diane are pregnant this season. Meredith, Rhea and Shelly are pregnant in real life, so the characters they play in prime time have to adapt their bodies and plots with media flair. One gets to have her baby as part of the story. She's married anyway, so that particular baby fits like a glove, right onto the hand of a married woman. The other two aren't married in their t.v. lives, so no network decisions have been made as yet. Last season Fay Furillo had a baby without being married, but in real life Barbara Bosson has children because she's married to the producer of *Hill Street Blues* who cast her as someone's ex-wife and someone's ex-lover because, as he said, "She's got the right look." Jane Pauley always plays herself; she had twins in real life and lately spends her time interviewing battered wives from Minneapolis right after Gene Shalitt interviews Farah Fawcett who reveals she is pregnant in real life though not married. She did have three children in her t.v. movie where she pretended to be a battered wife, and those children, the real ones, were the real reason the woman Farah pretended to be finally set her husband on fire and left home. Lately, Shelly is on a lot of talk shows, and she pulls her shoulders forward as if to ward off imagined blows. None of these t.v. women are battered. They are all happy women.

I have a new baby. No longer pregnant I drift through the house in an old white nightgown with faded flowers. My daughter asked me Thursday night if Elise said anything funny on this week's episode of *Family Ties*, and she complained that Carla is so mean to Diane on *Cheers* it just doesn't seem right. My daughter and my son kiss their new baby brother goodnight, they go up to bed, night after night, and suddenly it's autumn wherever we turn. Each window of our house finds a view of a colored tree, those wild extravaganzas, those hot torches flaming through the neighborhood. Every car ride to errands or lessons or jobs, we choose new trees as the best of the autumn season. We say it's all right the days are so gray, autumn colors lay against gray in a particularly splendid way. This is real life, the babies, the women who visit us each week on t.v., speaking of how much joy and work it is to make all these real and imaginary babies. All these babies just lying around, real enough to love and hold and change and watch, all the babies in autumn changing as fast as the trees. The babies will grow like trees, they will watch t.v. with their mothers, and it will be all right that for a while we lived so closely with television, its gracious light, its companionship, all those beta waves smoothing the rough edges, smoothing what's still raw and wounded in the mothers, what's still surprised and afraid in the babies.

SLOW CHILDREN CROSSING

For Larry and Peggy

Driving the mile to the ocean in August there's the sign: SLOW CHILDREN CROSSING, no punctuation, each word equivalent in size and importance. It's a warning, but I never slow down. Punishment waits for me on that road, my foot on the gas pedal, slow children suddenly in my line of vision, and I can't stop because I haven't rehearsed the punctuation of putting my foot on the brake. I've made the sign a picture not a warning: the line of children emerging from oak and bramble, crossing the road, disappearing into the hollow, the line unbroken, all day the tramp of children's feet across the beach road, slow and tan and a little sleepy. Last night my daughter asked Stephen, "Let's go the slow road way home, ok?" And I loved him because he didn't react in that dopey way adults do, the broad wink, the artistic pause, but instead said, "o.k." I believe next summer I will practice driving slowly, loving my children slowly, I will watch for SLOW CHILDREN CROSS-ING and I won't run down any of them, I will stop the car, lift Cassidy and Gabriel and Molly and Brendan out of the back seat, and we will walk slowly toward the dunes. We will become a gentle warning to others, a joyful warning about the pleasure of slowing down almost to a complete stop.

SUMMER WITH TWO VACATIONS: 1982

Now I have identified the Common Evening Primrose,
and the Bladder Campion,
colors first, then their clues of stem and leaf.
And now I have come home from the North Shore,
and the sun has burnt the grass, and my son's hair is
white, sprinklers are abandoned,
simple carnival rides for water.
"It's no good," my neighbor says,
his flowers flagging, small flames
only a week ago.

Now I have traveled east one more time;
without my lover I walk the bayside in the rain,
I find the simple scallop shell, the common brown,
and the white, not the hidden red hearted scallop
I dream of.

In Minnesota, I hear, the sun still shines,
the lawns are a curious shade of white,
but in Truro I identify shells and clouds
and my loneliness, and they are common
and I have been glad to feel such sadness
and to feel the weather so in unison with me.

ADMISSION

For Stephen

II. Will this trip appease a longing?
(stalling for time) The longing to go to China,
you mean?
Any longing.

        Project For a Trip To China, Susan Sontag

I.

Nothing prepared me for the surprise
of longing for you. Just fly east, I thought,
to the breaking edge of America, find some sun,
and the old comfort of silence and the empty bed.
Fly east, not so far as China, just far enough away
from acknowledged love,
the fierce uncertainties.

II.

Sometimes I think I'm a hard person,
harsh in spirit and language,
always breaking fast for the Atlantic
where nothing matters except sand,
where nothing matters but the search
for white stones, and the children
who skim past in waves: my only work
to catch them from the white foam before the tide
forces them to face the ocean, not the dunes.

III.

I can hold children in my hands,
I can slip white stones into pockets,
I can walk the bay side, quiet life in tide pools,
I can walk the ocean side, shuddering with solitude,
its dark complications.
I can do all this, and sleep alone, my body in fever
from too much sun, my eyes sorry to give up the light,
the half-read book.
I know all these things, the accomplishments
of a private life, yet the discovery
that you had come east with me
caught me up short, left me without breath.

Sometimes I think I know everything I want.
This time I was wrong, and admit without complacency
that the memory of your mouth turned my heart
like a red shell cast up
by the one wave I could not resist swimming in.

GREENLAND MUMMY

The best preserved of all the Greenland mummies is the baby boy mummy. He died quickly at six months of age, the snow his bed, his blanket, his death. So intact, he takes the breath of the archeologists: two white shells — lower teeth, cornsilk for hair, his tiny gloves, little blue starfish in the snow.

I make so much up. Haven't the time to study properly. I read two pages, pronounce a novelist "psychotic." I read one paragraph and know more than I ever wanted to know about the Greenland mummies.

The baby mummy wasn't wearing gloves; no shells, no cornsilk, a baby, not a doll. He was given to the snow after his mother died, so he couldn't wear gloves or the beautiful red over-alls or the soft deerskin cap with ear flaps, I made all that up when I was painting the baby mummy, I made it up so he would be warm.

Given to the snow because his mother died. The old rules hurt, not that the new rules are ideal. When the mother died in Greenland so many hundreds of years ago then her baby was put outside to die. And he became the best mummy, the one the scientists loved the best, because his little body froze so quickly, more quickly than the grown-up mummies and teen-age mummies who died with their clothes on. It is good he froze so quickly because the scientists are able to learn more from his tiny body. It is good to freeze quickly when your mother dies. It is good the rule was so clear: no aunts, no best friends of the mother may take the child; it is good to sleep in the snow when your mother dies. Maybe your aunt wouldn't love you enough, maybe your mother's best friend would love her own baby more. Who thought of such a dramatic rule in a country named Greenland? Who thought of Greenland anyway, that name of life, that huge island, and who thought of digging for mummies in the first place?

I don't know these answers. I don't read much lately, except what's assigned or what I struggle to see beyond the veil of tiredness. The baby wakes at night and I can't get back to sleep. I am sitting outside his door, my back straight against the doorframe. I am listening to each ragged breath he takes this month. I don't read much because of the baby. The baby is why I make things up. I love being up in the middle of the night with him; we watch the news, or old David Niven movies. We watched *Hawaii*, saw the circle of white, the halo/aura around Julie Andrews' head after she screamed and pulled on the tied-in-knots bedsheet and had her first baby. That is the first scene I ever remember seeing of childbirth. Later, a baby is put in the beautiful ocean to drown. I turned the t.v. off then because Joey was falling asleep. I wouldn't have let him watch that scene anyway.

The snow is almost gone from our backyard. My daughter made a mermaid without a face, with purple yarn hair; only the hair and the last part of the flipping tail remain. My daughter wants to be a mermaid when she grows up. Our baby will never sleep in the snow. I won't even let him go winter camping, even if it's the only way he can win merit badges in Boy Scouts. The baby will keep his snuggie on, and his blue mittens from Aunt Peggy, and his dark blue snowsuit from Jean, and his Harlequin socks from Pat and Tim, and the baby will sleep indoors always unless we move to the tropics.

The Greenland baby mummy has a beautiful and haunting face. I keep thinking of him, his small face, how he would fit in the hands and arms and heart of his mother who died.

I have been in mourning for children all over the world since our baby was born six months ago. The news from China, Africa, Lebanon; you can't send money fast enough, you can't melt the snow fast enough, or turn down the sun, or grow the crops or stop the bombs fast enough. Our new baby has done his job well, the job all babies are assigned: he has broken open my heart for the third time in my life, he has made me think of all these babies, alive, dead and dying. This is the work of babies; that is why there's no time to read, why I make everything up as I go along.

They are searching for more Greenland mummies. The group graves are confusing to the archeologists, so they hope to find more single graves. If they're lucky, they will stumble across another Greenland mummy baby. They hope the next one they find will have died even faster than the first. They long for what the snow does to babies.

That part may be wrong. They may have left Greenland by now. I will not be going to Greenland this year. I carry the picture of the baby mummy deep in me, like something I swallowed that has nothing to do with food. One paragraph, one picture is enough. Our baby is sleeping right now. He is warm, getting over his ailments of the last month. He is the light in our house. Someday I will tell him all these stories, the sad ones, the famines, the girl children left out to die, and the happy ones, the mermaid in the back yard, the women who love him, the gifts they've given. I am glad winter is ending and that the snow is almost gone.